To: Julian

Love Mom & Grant
From:
Hope you see it all

50 PLACES
TO SEE BEFORE YOU DiE
and 50 Places That Are a Lot More Fun

Nicholas Noyes

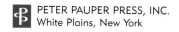

PETER PAUPER PRESS, INC.
White Plains, New York

TABLE OF CONTENTS

When the mother of all must-see lists, the Seven Wonders of the World, was created way back in 140 B.C., the push to overachieve—even on vacation—was set in motion. People immediately began suffering from vacation guilt, an affliction that plagues us still. "Sure, honey, I'd love to go spend a couple of weeks watching chariot races and drinking cheap Syracusian wine, but apparently we MUST SEE the Colossus of Rhodes . . . before we die."

And so it began: the rush to check things off a list. Been there, done that. If it's Tuesday, this must be the Mausoleum of Maussollos at Halicarnassus. Or is it the Hanging Gardens of Babylon? I can't tell in this light, and we've got an early chariot to catch in the morning.

After a while, you begin to wonder what happened to the fun.

Well, the fun is back. Here are 50 of the best attractions the world has to offer—and 50 places that will tease out that inner child . . . you know, the one with the naughty streak. If the Iditarod is too difficult to attend, the Idiotarod in Brooklyn may be easier to manage. Got a problem with the Running of the Bulls in Pamplona? Check out the Running of the Nudes! Can't make it to Stonehenge this year? Consider a jaunt to Nebraska, where Carhenge adds a kitschy spin to this relic from prehistory.

MORE FUN

★ 50 PLACES TO SEE BEFORE YOU DIE ★ 50 PLACES THAT ARE A LOT MORE FUN ★

It's not that the list makers don't have a point. The Empire State Building *is* pretty amazing. The Taj Mahal *can* give you goose bumps, and visiting the Great Barrier Reef *is* the experience of a lifetime (maybe a teeny bit fun, too). So it's all about balance. Keep the to-do list, but don't be afraid to put it away, relax, and do something a little silly, if not down-right goofy. What's the rush, anyway?

MUST-SEE:
Tournament of Roses Parade,
Pasadena, California, USA

Roses in rows

Pasadena has some great winter weather, and the city fathers wanted to make sure you knew about it. Since 1890, the city has held the Rose Parade on New Year's Day, as a salute to the town's winter blooms. The parade, a mixture of marching bands, elaborately decorated floral floats, and equestrian teams, now has a parade route audience of more than a million; many more watch the spectacle on television.

MORE FUN:
Doo Dah Parade,
Pasadena, California, USA

Mad marchers

Pasadena's goofier citizens and sillier visitors get to strut their stuff the weekend before Thanksgiving. The Doo Dah Parade offers a marvelously rendered spoof-counterpoint to the city's other parade, with over 100 groups marching, skipping, wandering, and napping over a mile-long parade route. Marchers have included a precision attaché case drill team, Clown Doctors from Outer Space, and the BBQ Hibachi & Grill Team.

MUST-SEE:

Iditarod,
Anchorage to Nome, Alaska, USA

There's no place like Nome.

In 1925, a relay of dog sleds raced diphtheria anti-toxin to Nome from Anchorage in time to prevent an outbreak of the disease.

These doggy heroes are remembered with an annual epic 1,150-mile race over much the same route, leaving Anchorage on the first Saturday in March, and arriving in Nome 10 to 17 days later. Braving temperatures below zero, sleds traverse a frozen landscape filled with rivers, forests, and tundra. A team of between 12 and 16 highly trained dogs pulls each sled.

Ìdiotarod, **Brooklyn, New York, USA**

Dogs for a day

In New York the dogs get to relax and watch more than 100 teams of five costumed "idiots" steer an often elaborately decorated shopping cart from Brooklyn to Manhattan by way of a number of checkpoints. Penalties are imposed for just about anything the judges choose, while Creative Bribery and Best Sabotage are encouraged with special awards. Rules are complex and arbitrary: "Any team wearing spandex is disqualified."

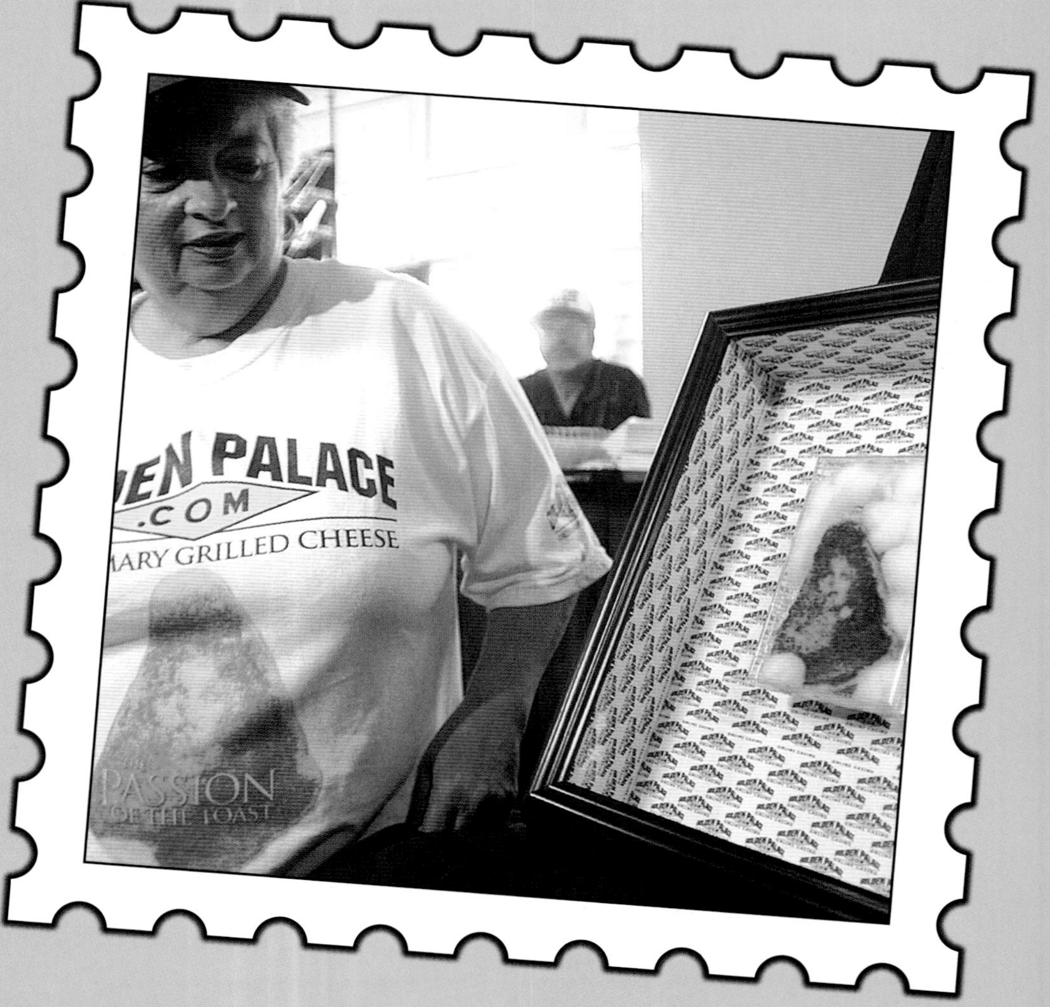
DEN PALACE
.COM
MARY GRILLED CHEESE
PASSION
OF THE TOAST

Shroud of Turin,
The Chapel of the Holy Shroud, Turin, Italy

Religious mystery

Curious visitors to Turin often go to the Chapel of the Holy Shroud, part of the Cattedrale di San Giovanni, home of the burial cloth that bears the image of a man thought by many to be Jesus Christ. They may be disappointed. Although artifacts related to the shroud are on display and a replica can be viewed, visitors will have to make do with proximity to the holy cloth, as it is shown to the public only on special occasions.

MUST-SEE:

MORE FUN:

Virgin Mary Grilled Cheese Sandwich,
GoldenPalace.com Headquarters, Austin, Texas, USA

Mystery sandwich

The sandwich, on which appears the apparent image of the Virgin Mary, was prepared in the 1990s and kept safe by its original owner. The Virgin Mary Grilled Cheese Sandwich was sold on eBay for $28,000 in 2004 and now has a home in the headquarters of GoldenPalace.com. The sandwich often tours with the Gurgitators of the International Federation of Competitive Eating, and is shown to the public at eating events—especially those in which grilled cheese sandwiches are featured.

MUST-SEE:

Poets' Corner,
Westminster Abbey, London, England

Dead poets' society

Westminster Abbey is where the United Kingdom's kings and queens are crowned and where they are buried. It also contains many monuments honoring the country's heroes. One of the most visited areas of the abbey is the Poets' Corner, where some of Britain's literary greats are entombed. This quiet spot is the final resting place of some of the most revered writers in the English language, including John Dryden, Lord Alfred Tennyson, Robert Browning, Dr. Johnson, Charles Dickens, and Rudyard Kipling.

Cowboy Poetry Festival,
Elko, Nevada, USA

Get along, li'l doggerel.

For a week in deep winter each year, this small town in Nevada, home of the Western Folk Life Center, hosts the National (as decreed by the U.S. Senate in the year 2000) Cowboy Poetry Gathering. In the popular imagination, the cowboy is a laconic figure whose utterances are crisp and to the point, but the cowboy poets here ride herd on a veritable stampede of versifying. When they're not declaiming, the bookish buckaroos and their fans watch performers from all over the world, bone up on elements of cowboy culture, such as wrangling and rope work, and occasionally visit the saloon.

More Fun

Bird-Watching,
Galápagos islands, Ecuador

Bring your binoculars.

Ever since Charles Darwin visited them in 1835, the Galápagos Islands have attracted bird-watchers. This is where Darwin observed the slight differences between closely related species of birds and began to formulate the theory of evolution. Part of modern Ecuador, the islands are still visited by scientists who study abundant and unique native wildlife found there. Tourists interested in bird-watching visit the islands to see penguins, frigate birds, pelicans, boobies, and many species of finch.

The Procession of Ducks in the Peabody Hotel, Memphis, Tennessee, USA

Duck!

The Peabody Hotel has had ducks living in the fountain of its lobby since the 1940s. Each morning the hotel Duckmaster leads the aquatic fowl across a red carpet to their daytime digs, accompanied by a Sousa march. Each evening he escorts them back to their luxury penthouse. There can be no more comfortable way to watch birds (unusual ones at that) than ensconced in a padded chair with the amenities of a good five-duck hotel at hand.

Smithsonian Institution,
Washington, D.C., USA

The nation's attic

The Smithsonian was founded in 1836 after a somewhat eccentric Englishman, James Smithson (who had never been to the United States), left money in his will to set up "an establishment for the increase and diffusion of knowledge among men." Based in Washington, D.C., the institution's collection is contained in 19 different museums and galleries. The 142 million items range from the *Spirit of St. Louis* airplane to (the original) Kermit the Frog.

Liberace Museum,
Las Vegas, Nevada, USA

Gilt-edged glamour

Containing what must be a generous percentage of the world's sequin supply, the Liberace Museum is the home of this beloved musician's cars, capes, and candelabra (not to mention one or two pianos), all of which have been covered in gold or glitter. Liberace was in the public eye from the early 1950s until his death in 1987, and the collection provides a glamorous glimpse of his unique career.

Glacier Bay National Park, Alaska

Icebergs are born here.

The national park, which covers over 5,000 square miles, is home to many glaciers. Here visitors can see calving icebergs; humpback, minke, and orca whales; and porpoises and seals in the bay. Moose and bears can be spotted onshore, while seabirds and eagles soar through the sky. Because there is no park access by road, a common way to get here is by sea. While the intrepid kayak in the bay, others take in the sights from the comfort of cruise-ship decks.

MUST-SEE

Ice Hotel, Quebec, Canada

Icy cool

Just outside Quebec City, this hotel, open from January until the April thaw, has everything you'd expect of a luxury winter resort. The difference: It's made entirely of ice. Guests need to layer up, but there are heated bathrooms and changing rooms for the heated pool. Beds are made of ice, but covered in furs and a mattress, and guests, exhausted after a day on snowmobiles, cross-country skis, or snowshoes, gladly retire to their cozy sleeping chambers.

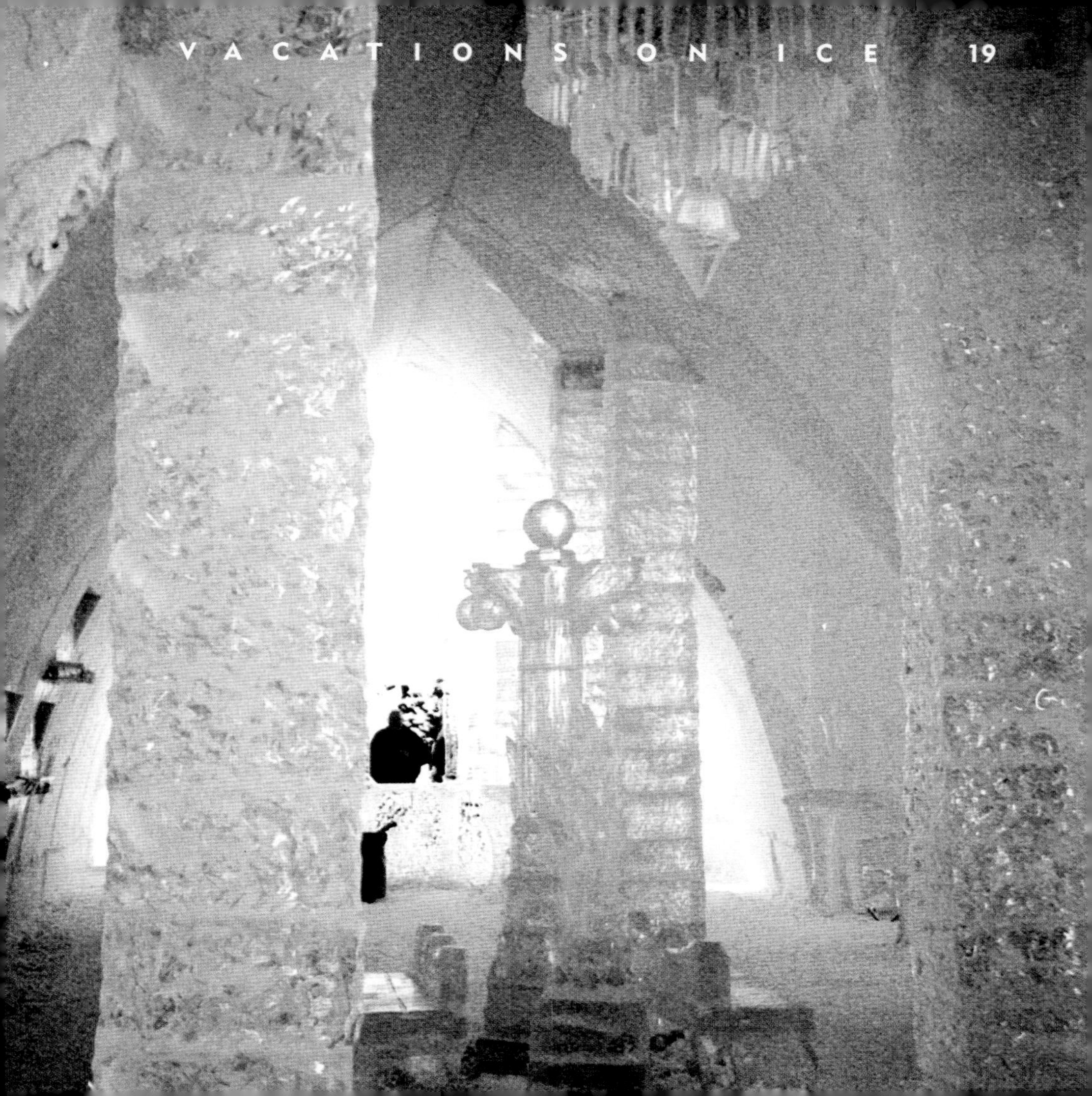

Angkor Wat, Cambodia

Jungle temple

Deep in the jungles of Southeast Asia, surrounded by a moat, is one of the world's great religious buildings. Built in the 12th century as a Hindu temple, Angkor Wat became a Buddhist place of worship some 300 years later. Remoteness and war have long kept all but the most intrepid visitors at bay, but the complex is now Cambodia's premier tourist destination. A depiction of the temple appears on Cambodia's flag and its currency.

MUST-SEE

Temple Tattoo Festival,
Wat Bang Phra, Thailand

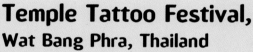

Temple tattoos

If the tattoo parlor at the mini-mall isn't quite edgy enough, you might consider getting some fresh ink at this Thai temple.

Each March, Thai people make a pilgrimage to a Buddhist temple west of Bangkok to acquire tattoos said to have mystical qualities. Wild scenes ensue when devotees who have been tattooed with an image of a tiger or a monkey go into a trance and imagine themselves to be those animals. The tattoos are believed to protect wearers from illness, ill fortune, and evil spirits.

Niagara Falls,
Border of USA and Canada

Honeymoon high jump

Niagara Falls is where people went to take the plunge: whether they planned to go over the falls in a barrel or embark on married life. This longtime honeymoon destination is located on the border between Canada and the United States, where Lake Erie drains into Lake Ontario. Attractions, other than watching 3,160 tons of water drop each second from the top of the falls, include donning plastic capes and taking a soggy voyage on the *Maid of the*

MUST-SEE

Canyoning,

Costa Rica

The end of your rope

You've just floated down some furious rapids, jumped into a pool deep in the Costa Rican jungle, and are preparing to rappel down a waterfall. That's the gentle sport of canyoning, the art of getting from A to B along a mountain river, going over (and not around) such obstacles as waterfalls, whirlpools, and rapids. Numerous companies offer guided introductions to canyoning in and around Costa Rica's numerous national parks.

MORE FUN

Running of the Bulls,
Pamplona, Spain

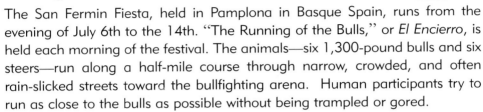

Rushing roulette

The San Fermin Fiesta, held in Pamplona in Basque Spain, runs from the evening of July 6th to the 14th. "The Running of the Bulls," or *El Encierro*, is held each morning of the festival. The animals—six 1,300-pound bulls and six steers—run along a half-mile course through narrow, crowded, and often rain-slicked streets toward the bullfighting arena. Human participants try to run as close to the bulls as possible without being trampled or gored.

Running of the Nudes,
Pamplona, Spain

The human race

In the days leading up to *El Encierro*, there is another race through the streets of Pamplona; spectators may find it equally as fascinating. As a protest against what they see as the cruelty of the bull run and bullfighting, animal lovers and activists have created their own annual tradition. Wearing red scarves (traditional garb of the bull runners), horns (traditional amongst the bulls), and very little else, these naked humans bounce and jiggle their way down the bulls' running course. While it is a great deal safer, there's probably still a chance of being trampled to death.

MUST-SEE:
Tsukiji Fish Market,
Tokyo, Japan

Cold fish

Arrive in the wee hours of the morning and witness the wonders of the deep slosh, wiggle, gasp, and squirm. Your visit offers you the opportunity to taste what you've seen. Neighborhood restaurants, from the very fancy to casual *kaiten* (conveyor belt sushi) joints, all offer the very freshest of fresh fish and are open early—if you can stomach raw fish first thing in the morning.

MORE FUN:
Cage Diving with Great White Sharks,
South Africa

Vacation chum

Whether or not you feel like breakfast, there's a chance that's exactly what a great white shark considers you to be. If you're swimming in a cage in the shark-filled ocean near Dyer Island off the coast of South Africa, in water chummed to attract these predators, you might feel you're being served up on a silver platter. Unlikely as it sounds, thousands of travelers every year do just this, in what has become among the latest in adventure tourism.

Cité de Carcassonne,
France

Medieval warfare

Carcassonne is the romantic ideal of a medieval city: its spires tower over the surrounding landscape. The walls date from the Middle Ages and were designed to withstand violent and sustained attacks by armies. Various siege techniques were used, including that of undermining the foundations. Among the most dramatic, however, was the use of siege engines, such as the *trebuchet*, to sling rocks the size of small (French) cars against the walls. The town endured many attacks and sieges, but it was seldom captured.

Must-see

Punkin' Chunkin' World Championship,
Sussex County, Delaware, USA

Pulping pumpkins

For the poet Keats, autumn was a "season of mists and mellow fruitfulness." In Sussex County, Delaware, it's time to smash some pumpkins. Nothing is mellow about the machines used to send pumpkins hurtling hundreds of feet into the air the weekend after Halloween. Competitors use devices that would make a medieval commander green with envy, from various traditional catapults to more modern apparatuses, which utilize compressed air.

More Fun

MUST-SEE:
The Changing of the Guard,
Buckingham Palace, London, England

"One of the sergeants looks after their socks."
(from "They're Changing Guard at Buckingham Palace," by A. A. Milne)

Colorful costumes, classic tunes, precise footwork, and a bit of yelling are key ingredients of London's favorite military pageant, which takes place most mornings during the summer and less frequently at other times. With the pomp and formality that is a British military tradition, the soldiers guarding the Queen (or often just her house) are relieved by another group as a military band plays.

MORE FUN:
Corn Palace,
Mitchell, South Dakota, USA

Changing of the corn

Mitchell's Corn Palace (the world's only one) is a convention hall built in 1921. Its unusual domes and minarets were added later. What gives the palace its name and makes it unique are the mosaics on its walls, created using South Dakota corn (and other grains). The murals are changed every year in the spring and finished by the beginning of fall, at which time, locals note, the Mitchell becomes the home of the world's largest bird feeder.

MUST-SEE:

U.N. Headquarters, NYC, New York, USA

International smorgasbord

The U.N.'s headquarters in New York City was completed in 1950. Since then the building has been grudgingly accepted by New Yorkers, who feel its inhabitants are unfairly exempt from city parking rules. Visitors can take a guided tour, or book a table at the Delegates' Dining Room, which features a menu of world cuisines. Because the U.N. occupies international territory, a visit there allows you to leave the U.S. without leaving Manhattan Island.

MORE FUN:

Epcot Center,
Walt Disney World,
Orlando, Florida, USA

World party

A vision of the future, albeit with a great deal more animatronics than occur in everyday life—even today—Epcot is a celebration of technology and world culture. Here you can visit countries as envisioned by Disney's imagineers without the hassle of multiple plane journeys, language barriers, and funny currencies. On the other hand, you will likely come across people from countries other than your own: Disney's Epcot Center hosts millions of visitors from around the world every year.

New Year's Eve Celebration,
Times Square, New York City, New York, USA

MUST-SEE:

The ball drops.

The "Crossroads of the World" is a popular place to see in the New Year. If you choose to spend the evening of December 31st watching the Waterford crystal ball drop in Times Square, you'll be in the company of an estimated three-quarters of a million other people—so don't expect your friends and family to be able to pick you out of the crowd if they're watching on TV.

MORE FUN:

Burning of Zozobra,
Santa Fe, New Mexico, USA

Up in smoke

Santa Fe's fiesta, a September pageant, begins with the ritual burning of Zozobra. Old Man Gloom, a 50-foot-tall effigy, is symbolic of all the negative aspects of the previous year and is often stuffed with documents having bad associations: divorce decrees, old tax demands, etc. Out with the old, in with the new. The fiesta dates from 1712; local artist William Howard Shuster instituted the gloom-banishing Zozobra burning in 1924.

The Kremlin, Moscow, Russia

Spook central

MUST-SEE

The fortified heart of Russian government, both under the tsars and the Soviets, the Kremlin is a complex that contains government buildings and residences of Russian leaders, as well as churches and other religious buildings (some with the onion domes often associated with traditional Russia). Many of the buildings are now open to tourists, but some remain closed to public scrutiny. Move along, comrade, nothing to see here.

MORE FUN:
International Spy Muse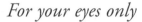um,
Washington, D.C., USA

For your eyes only

Spooks, sneaks, assassins, and other undercover operatives are celebrated in this District museum, containing artifacts of the world's long history of spying, from the Greeks and Romans to the present day. The collection includes the "Kiss of Death," a working gun concealed in a lipstick tube, the Enigma Cipher machine, buttonhole cameras, and a radio transmitter hidden in the heel of a shoe. The museum shop sells spy gadgets for would-be James Bonds.

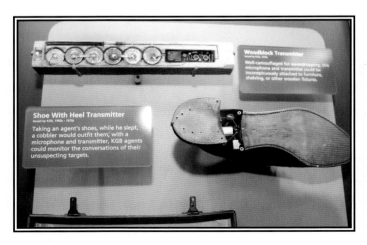

MUST-SEE:
The Tower of London, England

The bloody tower

Built by William the Conqueror, this Norman castle has offered protection to London (and kept an eye on its inhabitants) and has served as a prison, an armory, a barracks, the home of the crown jewels, an execution site, a zoo, and a torture chamber. Some of the Tower's famous former prisoners include Ann Boleyn (who was beheaded there), Sir Walter Raleigh, Guy Fawkes, and Nazi Rudolph Hess. Today, the tower is home to Beefeater guards and their families—and a pampered flock of ravens.

Alcatraz, San Francisco, California, USA

No escape

Former U.S. federal penitentiary Alcatraz (a.k.a. "The Rock") was the home of such notorious prisoners as Al Capone, "Machine Gun" Kelly, and Robert Stroud, the "Birdman of Alcatraz." Designed to be escape-proof, the prison employed the most modern security innovations of its day and was surrounded by the chilly waters of San Francisco Bay. In its 29 years of operation, there were only 14 escape attempts; officially, none was successful. Closed by Attorney General Robert F. Kennedy in 1963, Alcatraz is now run by the U.S. National Park Service. Visitors can tour the island, the prison, and a museum and listen to an award-winning audio tour, featuring interviews with former inmates and corrections officers.

MUST-SEE:

St. Burchardi Church, Halberstadt, Germany

Organ solo

On an organ in a church in the German city of Halberstadt, "As Slow as Possible," a composition by American avant-garde composer John Cage, is played at a leisurely pace. Just how slowly? The plan is for the piece to be performed over 639 years. Whether it is actually "possible" remains to be seen. In the meantime, excited fans gather every couple of years when a note changes.

Air Guitar World Championship, Oulu, Finland

All in the wrist

If your time is limited, you could take in the performances at the world air-guitar competition in northern Finland. Performers and aficionados of the guitar-miming art form travel from all over the world to be part of the festivities, and competition is fierce. The championship is dedicated to world peace: "All the bad things in the world would disappear if all people played the air guitar," say the organizers.

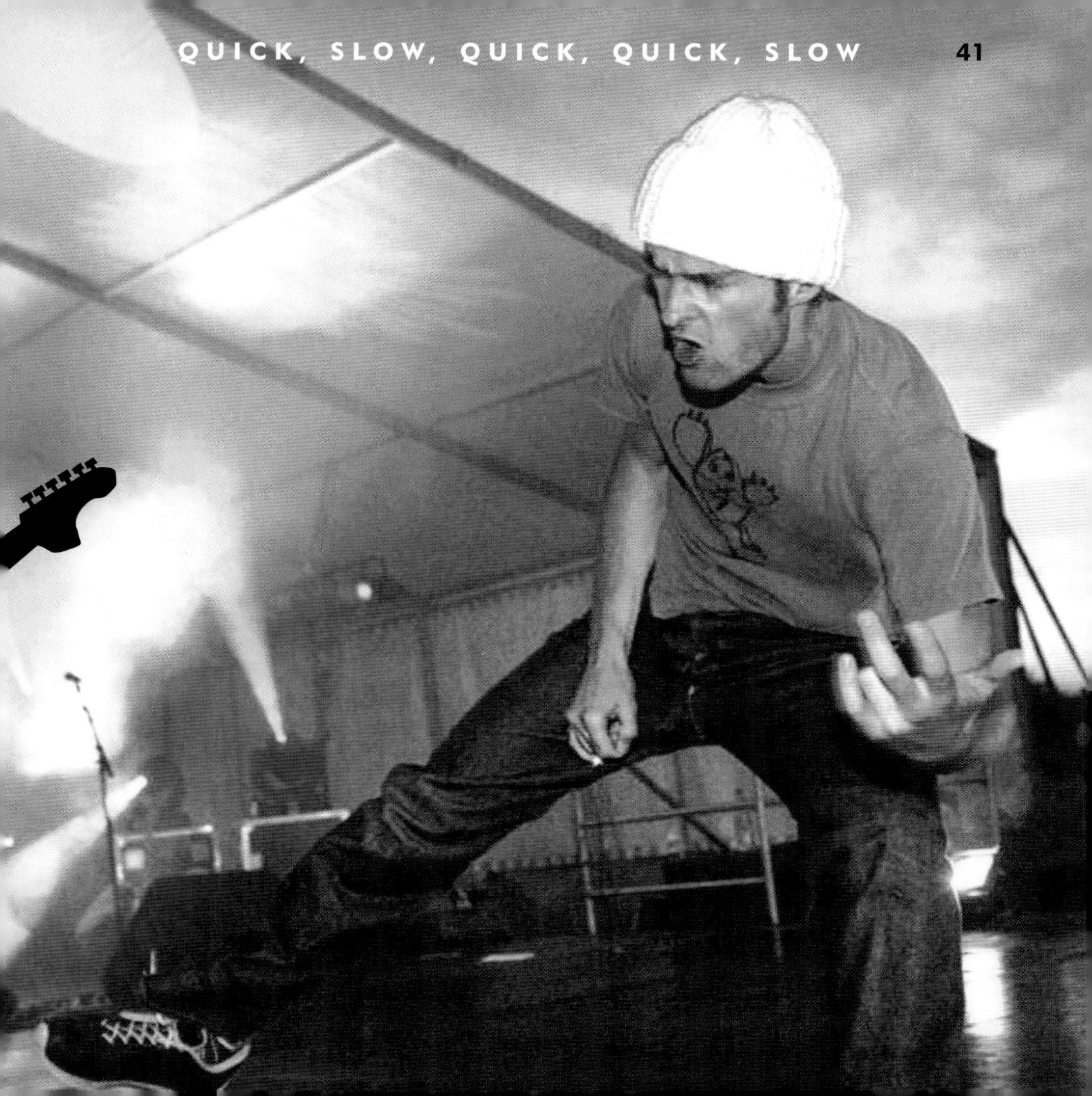

Eiffel Tower, **Paris, France**

Ooh la la

Built for the 1889 *Exposition Universelle*, this iconic symbol of the City of Light was originally supposed to stand for only 20 years. That it has stood for well over a century as one of Paris's foremost attractions is proof of the hardiness of the 19th-century iron construction technology. Over the years it has been used as an advertising billboard, a military lookout, and for radio and television transmissions. The tower receives about six million visitors a year.

Must-see

MORE FUN:

The Parachute Jump
"New York's Eiffel Tower,"
Coney island, Brooklyn, New York, USA

Fuhgeddaboudit

Originally created for the 1939 World's Fair, the Parachute Jump moved to Coney Island in the 1940s. Although the jump is no longer operational, the landmark structure is adjacent to the myriad attractions of Coney Island: the annual mermaid parade, the July 4th hot dog eating competition, the minor league Brooklyn Cyclones, the infamous Cyclone roller coaster, the New York Aquarium, and access to the world's most famous hot dogs. Since July of 2006, the Jump has been illuminated at night, a proud beacon of Coney Island culture.

Taj Mahal, Agra, India

Endless love

Completed in 1654, the Taj Mahal was built by the Emperor Shah Jahan as a mausoleum for his wife. Set off by formal gardens, the marble tomb with its distinctive dome is also a monument to refined elegance. The Taj is one of India's greatest tourist attractions—and a commemoration of marital love.

The Trump Taj Mahal Casino Resort, Atlantic City, New Jersey, USA

50 PLACES TO SEE BEFORE YOU DIE ★ 50 PLACES THAT ARE A LOT MORE FUN ★

MORE FUN

Lost weekend

The Taj features a 161,000-square-foot casino with more than 4,000 slot machines and 200 gaming tables. There are 15 spots for dining and drinking and a 1,250-room hotel, which attracts such top entertainers as Michael Bolton and Kenny Rogers. The resort's owner, Donald Trump, is considered something of an expert on marriage.

The Louvre, Paris, France

Gilded palace

A royal castle was first built on this site in the 12th century, and the French have been rebuilding and adding to it ever since. (The most recent addition is I. M. Pei's stunning glass pyramid in the courtyard, which serves as one of the entrances to the museum.) With over six million visitors a year, the Louvre is one of the world's most loved museums. The building houses some 35,000 works of art, including Leonardo da Vinci's *La Gioconda*, aka the *Mona Lisa*.

MUST-SEE

Paris Sewer Museum,
Paris, France

Going underground

Paris's sewers date from the 14th century, and these underground passages are home to some mysterious goings-on. As recently as 2004, Paris police on a training exercise came across an underground cinema here, equipped with a bar. But of course! While it is no longer possible to tour the sewers of Paris by boat, as was the case until the 1960s, you can catch a glimpse of this underground world by visiting the Paris Sewer Museum, located, naturally, in a Parisian sewer.

The Great Barrier Reef, Australia

Dive in an underwater paradise.

The reef, a living underwater forest of coral stretching for 1,600 miles along Australia's northeast coast, is one of nature's wonders. Multicolored fish, aquatic mammals, and underwater flora make their home amongst the coral; the reef is often described as the only living organism visible from space. Here amongst the coral you might see leatherback turtles, dugongs (a cousin of the manatee), any number of shark species, colorful fish, and over 400 different kinds of coral. (You might even find Nemo.) To get a better look, visitors can explore the tropical waters in glass-bottom boats, from observation decks or helicopters, or by using scuba or snorkeling equipment.

MUST-SEE

World Bog-Snorkeling Championship,
Llanwrtyd Wells, Wales

Snorkel in a mud-filled hole.

Contestants explore the delicate ecosystem of a chilly Welsh bog close up by plunging headfirst into its murky depths and snorkeling the simple there-and-back course (using flipper power but without resorting to actual swimming). Bog snorklers are awarded prizes for the best time, as well as for fancy dress, before repairing to the local pub.

MORE FUN

MUST-SEE:
Westminster Kennel Club Dog Show,
New York City, New York, USA

Top dogs

The Westminster show has been held at Madison Square Garden or one of its antecedents since 1877. Every February, up to 2,500 dogs attend, representing the best of 150 breeds, from tiny diva dogs you can fit in your purse to brawny working canines. The dogs are judged by the rigorous standards of the American Kennel Club, and the winners often go on to a profitable retirement as breeding animals.

MORE FUN:
Tompkins Square Halloween Dog Parade,
New York City, New York, USA

Hipster pooches

Mutts (along with some slumming purebreds) with attitudes and fabulous costumes parade in this late October event on New York's Lower East Side. Here the dogs are not judged on how close they come to Kennel Club ideals, but on the flair with which they wear clothes. Best Costume prizes are awarded for large and small dogs, dog teams, dogs with kids, and dog-and-owner combos.

The Hermitage,
St. Petersburg, Russia

Tsars' palace

Long the winter home of the tsars (and first to be stormed by the crowd when the Russian Revolution began in 1917), the Winter Palace was once the byword for regal living. The rococo building, completed in 1762, is now part of the Hermitage Museum, Russia's extraordinary collection of art and artifact. Hermitage holdings include paintings by old masters such as Titian, Raphael, da Vinci, and Michelangelo, and 20th-century artists, including Picasso, Gauguin, and Matisse, plus Russian icons and Fabergé jewelry and enamelware.

Must-see

Graceland,
Memphis, Tennessee, USA

King's castle

Since his death in 1977, Elvis's home has become a museum, and in 2006 it was declared a National Historic Landmark. It is also a pilgrimage site for the King's many fans, who visit the mansion to view its collection of Elvis-related materials. Rooms of the house remain unchanged from the time of Presley's reign; you'll find his Cadillacs both pink and black, motor bikes, and memorabilia from his music and film career.

More Fun

MUST-SEE:
Henley Royal Regatta,
Henley-on-Thames, England

Refined river race

Crews from all over the world compete at this regatta established in 1839. While the Eights race upon the river Thames during the first week of July, the action worth watching is amongst the spectators. The aristocratic and merely rich alike strap on their best blazers and loudly support their schools, while quaffing Pimm's Cup, a mysterious gin-based cocktail. The exclusive Stewards' Enclosure is the ultimate place to see and be seen; here a strict dress code applies. Men must wear blazers or suits; women wear dresses and even hats.

MORE FUN:
Henley-on-Todd Regatta,
Alice Springs, Australia

Dry river run

Alice Springs, a town in the Northern Territory, is very hot and very dry. The Todd River, which runs through town, has everything a river needs except, for the most part, water. This doesn't stop the annual "bat rice," as pronounced by locals, which is run, literally, by crews whose feet stick out of the bottom of the boat. There's no dress code as such, but you're going to feel pretty silly if you're not outfitted as a Viking or at least a pirate.

The Coliseum, Rome, Italy

Roman gladiators!

Constructed around A.D. 72 during the reign of the Emperor Vespasian, Rome's Coliseum was, for more than 500 gory years, the site of battle reenactments and executions by wild beasts, as well as everyday bloody combat by skilled gladiators, who often fought to the death. Events such as these were wildly popular, and the Coliseum held over 50,000 spectators. In the Middle Ages it was used as housing, retail space, a cemetery, and a fort. Today the familiar oval amphitheater is one of the world's best-known historic sites.

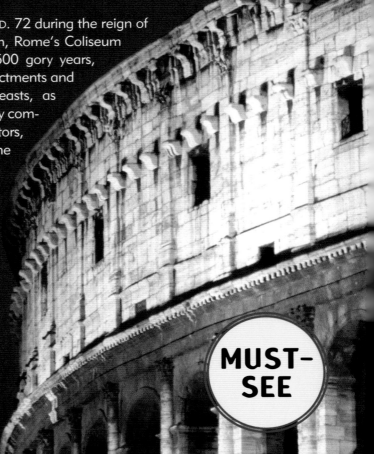

MUST-SEE

La Tomatina, **Valencia, Spain**

Gladiatorial gazpacho

Every year in late August nearly 140 tons of tomatoes are trucked into the town of Buñol, and for a couple of hours the town's inhabitants (and many visitors) pelt each other with the red, juicy vegetables. (By the way, they're technically fruits.) No quarter is asked for, and none is given. If you attend the enormous, messy battle, bring your swimming goggles—all that tomato juice can sting the eyes and ruin your fun.

MUST-SEE:

Stonehenge, Wiltshire, England

This rocks!

The massive stones of this circle stand in isolation on the Salisbury Plain as they have for millennia; Stonehenge is as mysterious as it is renowned. The exact purpose of the prehistoric construction is unknown (although it is thought to be a calendar, and it is aligned with the rising sun of the winter and summer solstice). And as is traditional (but now with more ice cream and souvenirs), travelers come to wonder at this mystery, revel in its ancient power, and share crackpot theories as to its origin.

MORE FUN:

Carhenge, Alliance, Nebraska, USA

This rolls!

In western Nebraska near the town of Alliance stands a less mysterious (but rather exact) version of Stonehenge created out of junked American cars painted gray. People, for instance, know that a man named Jim Reinders built Carhenge, and it was finished in 1987. And although his neighbors were a little unsure of exactly what he was up to, his circle of cars is an effective tribute to the older henge, attracting local druids (who knew?) during the summer and winter solstice, along with other visitors.

Alhambra,
Granada, Spain

Spanish dream

The dreamy courtyards of the Alhambra (or Red Castle), home to the Islamic rulers of Granada, are part of a complex of buildings representing the zenith of Moorish architecture on the Iberian Peninsula. With a view of the often snow-clad Sierra Nevada, set in orange groves and cooled by elaborate irrigation systems, the citadel is Spain's quintessential castle.

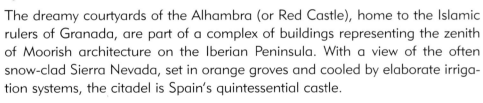

Rhinefield House,
Hampshire, England

English oasis

Built in the 1880s, this elegant country seat, constructed in the Jacobean style, is nestled in England's beautiful New Forest. A honeymoon in Spain inspired the owner to meticulously re-create the architecture of the Alhambra in her home, using materials from the Islamic world and artisans from Spain. The result was the Alhambra Smoking Room. Rhinefield House is now a luxury hotel, and although it is now a nonsmoking facility, its Alhambra, recently restored, is in use as part of the restaurant.

Temple of Apollo,
Delphi, Greece

Classical visions

Wondering if the time is right to lay waste to your enemies' cities? Until the 4th century A.D., the Oracle of Apollo at Delphi is where princes, generals, and athletes went to learn what they should do next. The ancients took the phrase "make of it what you will" to heart and generally went ahead with whatever mayhem they anticipated, only later to discover the hidden catch in the Delphic pronouncement. Visitors to Delphi today can visit the temple of Apollo and other classical remains.

Gobbler's Knob, Punxsutawney, Pennsylvania, USA

The shadow knows

Other soothsayers may bring you news-to-be, but only Punxsutawney Phil tells you about the weather. Since 1886, groundhogs have been predicting the course of the winter in the western Pennsylvania town of Punxsutawney. Midwinter high jinks surround the rodent weather forecast as eager crowds gather at Gobbler's Knob on Groundhog Day (February 2nd), to see whether this national institution will see his own shadow.

MUST-SEE:
Sistine Chapel, Vatican City, Rome, italy

When in Rome

The Sistine Chapel, where the College of Cardinals sits to elect each new pope, was built in the 15th century. As sometimes happens, it took a few years to get the ceiling painted. Michelangelo, commissioned by Pope Julius II, worked on the Sistine Chapel for several years, completing his frescoes in 1512. The ceiling depicts scenes from the book of Genesis, including the famous image of Adam receiving life by the hand of God.

MORE FUN: Graffiti Hall of Fame,
East Harlem, New York City, New York, USA

A rose in Spanish Harlem

Part of the hip-hop culture that exploded out of New York in the late '70s and early '80s, graffiti artists have gone on to successful careers in advertising and graphic design and as gallery artists. An otherwise unprepossessing playground in upper Manhattan, close to where it all began, is home to the Graffiti Hall of Fame, founded in 1980 to give artists a legal outlet for their work. New murals are added each year in June.

MUST-SEE:
Bath,
Somerset, England

Taking the waters

The Romans appreciated the merits of a good soak, and so when they discovered hot springs in the west of England, they promptly built a temple to the goddess Minerva and brought along their *anatriculae elasticae* (rubber duckies). Bathing went through some lean times during the Middle Ages, but by the 18th century, having a dip was fashionable again. The city of Bath was extensively developed in the Georgian era, which is when the renowned Royal Crescent Hotel and Bath House Spa was built, and was home to Jane Austen in the 19th century.

MORE FUN:
Bathtub Race and Nanaimo Marine Festival,
British Columbia, Canada

Good clean fun

"Bath time fun" cannot be seriously defined until you account for the World Championship Bathtub Race. These racers don't push boats around a bathtub with their toes; they take bathtubs, make them seaworthy, and attach outboard motors. Since 1967, "tubbers" have raced around a 36-mile course, first in Vancouver's harbor and lately beginning and ending in Nanaimo, at speeds in excess of 30 miles an hour (or 20 or so knots).

The Old Course, St. Andrews, Scotland

Golfing tradition

MUST-SEE

Golf was being played on the Old Course at St. Andrews by the 16th century, although players may have had to share the links with footballers and locals raising rabbits. Now dedicated solely to golf, the course attracts players from all over the world. Once on the links they have to contend with notoriously difficult play, making sure to avoid the 112 different bunkers (with reassuring names like Hell, The Coffins, Cat's Trap, and Lion's Mouth). The British Open is played here approximately every five years.

Hans Merensky Estate, Phalaborwa, South Africa

Golfing safari

MORE FUN

If someone talks about "Lion's Mouth" on the luxurious Hans Merensky Estate, don't blithely assume they're referring to a bunker. Your life may depend on it. What is possibly the world's most dangerous golf course abuts the Kruger National Park Game Reserve. Large fauna including giraffes, elephants, and lions have been known to wander the greens (in defiance of club rules), and with lurking hippos and crocodiles, the water hazards live up to their name.

Aspen,
Colorado, USA

Ski cool

A former mining town turned counter-culture hangout in the '60s, Aspen has hit pay dirt as a ski destination. The onetime home of singer John Denver and gonzo-journalist Hunter S. Thompson is now a favorite with jet-set skiers, millionaire second home owners, and celebs who spend as much time shopping luxury boutiques and dining out as on the slopes.

Must-see

Ski Dubai, Dubai, United Arab Emirates

Ski hot

There's something a little otherworldly about Dubai, where hi-tech meets outrageous architectural fantasy, which may be why there are plans to build a spaceport just outside of town. When temperatures hit 100 in this corner of the Arabian Desert, it's good to know you can go skiing in the world's largest indoor ski mountain with five different slopes (including the world's only indoor black diamond run). Temperatures are kept a few degrees below freezing, and up to 1,500 people can ski at the same time.

MUST-SEE:
Tour de France, France
France on 10,000 calories a day

Since 1903, the Tour de France has generated fanaticism amongst the cycling nations of Europe and (somewhat) polite bafflement in the rest of the world. By any standard, it is one of the supreme tests of human abilities. During the three weeks of "le Tour," cyclists cover 2,300 miles at an average speed of 25 miles an hour, mountains notwithstanding. The race is viewed by as many as 15 million people standing alongside the course.

MORE FUN:
The Painted Naked Cyclists of the Summer Solstice Parade, Seattle, Washington, USA
Tour de no-pants

The origins of the tradition are hazy, but naked cyclists have been part of the summer solstice parade in the Fremont section of Seattle since the early 1990s. Despite early controversy, they are now firmly part of the parade tradition, and as many as a couple of hundred (that's a *lot* of naked velocipedists) lead the parade, wearing nothing but helmets, shoes, and usually body paint.

Bateaux-Mouches, Paris, France

A river runs through it.

For many, it is the perfect way to see Paris. A journey up and down the Seine allows one to see the sights—the Eiffel Tower, Notre Dame, the Louvre, and the Musée D'Orsay—without contending with the hustle and bustle of Paris traffic. A popular tradition in this ancient city, Bateaux-Mouches have been introducing the City of Light from the river since the 1940s.

MUST-SEE

Atlantis Submarine Tour,
Waikiki, Hawaii, USA

Undersea tourism

Atlantis Adventures Company boats leave from Waikiki, taking passengers to the company's fleet of submarines. On a 45-minute tour inside the world's largest nonmilitary submarine, passengers see a downed airliner, shipwrecks, artificial reefs, sea turtles, sharks, and colorful tropical fish. So far they have not had to battle a giant squid, but it is clearly only a matter of time.

MORE FUN

Vineyard Tour,
Napa Valley, California, USA

On the vine

A journey up Highway 29 north of San Francisco takes you through the wine-producing Napa Valley. Here you can sample the best in American wines, stopping at world-famous vineyards like Robert Mondavi's, taking in a boutique winery or two, and see sparkling wine made using the Champagne method. Chic restaurants, like the French Laundry, cater to visiting oenophiles and local gourmets.

Must-see

Guinness Tour,
St. James's Gate Brewery,
Dublin, Ireland

Good for you

Guinness has been making beer at their Dublin brewery since 1759, and visitors are welcome at its specially designed Storehouse. This eight-story building—"the largest pint in the world"—is built in the shape of a giant glass of Guinness. Visitors learn about the history of the brand and the brewing process before ending up at the top floor Gravity Bar, where they can sample the product and enjoy panoramic views of the Irish capital.

More Fun

MUST-SEE:

JFK Space Center, Cape Canaveral, Florida, USA

Ad astra per aspera (To the stars through difficulties)

America's space agency, NASA, was formed in 1958 and has been fulfilling its mission statement, "to advance human exploration, use, and development of space," ever since. Astronauts boldly go into space from the John F. Kennedy Space Center near Cape Canaveral, Florida. The Visitor Complex is a popular tourist destination, with museums, IMAX theaters, and bus tours. The public can also watch launches of certain missions from the space center.

International UFO Museum and Festival, Roswell, New Mexico, USA

Alien encounters

In 1947, aliens crash-landed near this town in New Mexico—or so they say. The Roswell Museum (and research library) has been countering the government's conspiracy of silence since 1991. The museum contains exhibits about the original Roswell incident, as well as phenomena such as UFO sightings, abductions, and crop circles. A July festival, held partly in the museum, brings the inquisitive and eccentric together each year to attend lectures, meet experts in the field, dance, and listen to live music.

More Fun

White Water Rafting,
Grand Canyon, Arizona, USA

Shoot the rapids.

Ever since Major John Wesley Powell successfully navigated the Colorado River in 1869, people have been floating through the unique landscape of the Grand Canyon in boats. Today, any number of commercial companies take tourists down the river in a variety of craft, from small dinghies to large motorized rafts, which are practically luxurious, if your definition of luxury includes becoming sopping wet.

Canyon Ranch Tucson,
Arizona, USA

Desert spa

This spa in the Sonoran Desert north of Tucson is anything but Spartan. For those who prefer that the bubbling waters surrounding them be heated and spumed by a Jacuzzi, this is the perfect adventure holiday. With an emphasis on healthy living, the ranch allows visitors to recharge their batteries by taking part in a variety of activities, such as yoga, swimming, and bike riding, all while enjoying luxurious accommodations and spa cuisine.

The Great Pyramid of Giza, Egypt

Mysterious necropolis

The Great Pyramid of Giza, tomb of the pharaoh Khufu, was completed around 2600 B.C. The builders, despite using only human power and having nothing but simple tools, completed the pyramid in, by some estimates, a relatively snappy 20 years. Although the pyramids have been intensively studied, from their massive bulk to the hidden treasure chambers within, they remain profoundly mysterious. The Great Pyramid is the last remaining of the ancient Seven Wonders of the World.

MUST-SEE

U.S. Open Sandcastle Competition,
San Diego, California

A bucket and a dream

In the sandy wastes on the outskirts of San Diego known as Imperial Beach, teams in both pro and amateur categories compete for cash prizes using only human power and a bucket and shovel. Some people never get over the lure of digging in the sand. In a competition that's anything but child's play, sand architects have only five hours in which to build their wonders, ranging from traditional castles to depictions of pop culture icons.

MORE FUN

MUST-SEE:

Great Wall, China

Keeping barbarians at bay

The world's longest man-made structure, China's Great Wall stretches about 4,000 miles and is constructed, at various points, out of bricks, stones, wood, and compacted earth. Parts of the wall were built as early as 500 B.C. (only to be rebuilt many times), and the wall was still in use 1,000 years later. Designed to keep out foreign invaders, it now has the opposite effect, attracting legions of tourists who visit the restored areas.

MORE FUN:

El Capitan,
Yosemite Valley National Park, California, USA

Totally awesome wall

Yosemite is a popular vacation destination, but for rock climbers, a visit is more akin to a pilgrimage. Lost Arrow, Cathedral Spire, and Half Dome are all walls that every rock climber aspires to conquer. But the greatest challenge is El Capitan, 3,000 feet of vertical granite rising from the valley floor. Today's climbers take just two or three days to get up "El Cap," tying themselves into the rock face at night to get some rest.

Empire State Building,
New York City, New York, USA

Touching the clouds

Since it was built in the early years of the Great Depression, the 1,453-foot-high Empire State Building has fascinated the world (and a certain giant monkey). Although early plans to incorporate a dirigible docking station atop the roof were abandoned, visitors can take an elevator to the 1,000-foot-high observation deck, which on a clear day affords 50-mile views in all directions. Three-and-a-half million people a year visit the observatory.

Skywalk,
Grand Canyon, Arizona, USA

Walking on air

A three-hour drive from Las Vegas, the Skywalk is the region's newest tourist attraction. Built by the Hualapai, a Native American tribe, and opened to the public in March 2007, the Skywalk is a horseshoe-shaped structure extending 65 feet over the rim of the Grand Canyon. With nothing but glass beneath their feet, the view for the visitor is 4,000 feet straight down. Visitors wear paper booties to protect the see-through floor of the skywalk.

Antarctica

Frozen continent

Once the home of penguins (and not much else), this frigid continent has, since the beginning of the 20th century, hosted explorers and scientists. And it's now the tourists' turn. Flights leave from Australia and fly over snowfields, but for a closer look, visitors arrive on ships, cruise the Antarctic waters, and make brief shore trips during the summer when temperatures reach 50°F, positively balmy compared to winter lows which can reach a benumbing -112°F.

Harbin Ice Festival,
Harbin, China

Crystal city

A million people visit Harbin in northern China during the New Year holiday, attracted by the annual winter ice festival. In this city, long occupied by Russia, fantastic palaces, exotic temples, and vast cathedrals are created by ice artisans from around the world. Providing a cheery break during the long, dark winter, the dazzling ice city is colorfully lit from within. In keeping with the icy theme, the traditional snack served winter visitors is ice cream.

MORE FUN

MUST-SEE:
Teatro alla Scala, Milan, Italy

Maximum opera

If opera has a home, perhaps it is at La Scala. Ever since 1778, the Milanese and others have been spending evenings with *Don Giovanni*, *Carmen*, and the occasional *Fledermaus* in this neoclassical opera house. Here, in the 19th century, Verdi premiered many of his operas, while in the 20th Toscanini conducted its orchestra. Audiences are notoriously tough, but meeting the approval of the *loggione* ("cheap" seats) is often a riotous achievement.

More Fun

The Grand Ole Opry,
Nashville, Tennessee, USA

A night at the Opry

The Grand Ole Opry started out as a weekly show on a Nashville radio station in the 1920s, featuring the likes of Minnie Pearl and the Possum Hunters. Today's performers stand in a wooden circle cut from the stage floor of the Ryman Auditorium, the Opry's former longtime home, treading the same boards as legends such as Hank Williams and Johnny Cash.

MUST-SEE:
Statue of Liberty,
New York City,
New York, USA

Harbor beauty

For over a century, this steadfast lady in green has presided over New York Harbor, welcoming ship-borne visitors to the USA. Each year more than four million of the overtired, the cranky, the yearning to get back to the hotel take the boat ride to Liberty Island to visit France's memorable gift to America and see the 151-foot-tall statue close up.

MORE FUN:
LEGOLAND,
Carlsbad, California, USA

Another brick

In LEGOLAND's Miniland USA, New York's most famous attractions—including the **Statue of Liberty**—are re-created in miniature, using the company's cunningly crafted (but dangerous if you step on them in bare feet) plastic bricks. Central Park, the Met Life building, Grand Central Terminal, and the Empire State Building are all there. Their Statue of Liberty stands close to 12 feet tall, and is made up of almost 123,000 individual pieces weighing a total of 512 pounds. Standing in a two-million-gallon lagoon, LEGO Lady Liberty welcomes visitors from large to small.

MUST-SEE:
Forbidden City, Beijing, China
Emperors' palace

The Forbidden City, on the northern edge of Tiananmen Square in Beijing, consists of a palace complex, traditionally said to have 999 buildings. When it was home of the Chinese emperor, only the favored were allowed within; access by the hoi polloi was forbidden. It is now the home of the Palace Museum, which supervises ongoing restoration. The site covers 178 acres and is protected by a wall and a moat.

MORE FUN:
Forbidden Gardens, Katy, Texas, USA
Palatial gardens

Deep in the heart of Texas is a little bit of China. The Forbidden Gardens, located in the Houston-area city of Katy, Texas, provide a guided tour around China in the course of an afternoon. Here is the Terra Cotta army at one-third scale, the Summer Palace—the Chinese emperors' vacation retreat—and the Forbidden City, which at one-twentieth the size of the real thing, still has a 40,000-square-foot footprint.

MUST-SEE:
Lipizzaner Horses,
Spanish Riding School,
Vienna, Austria

Dancing horses

The much-schooled stallions of the Spanish Riding School and their equally well-trained riders perform with a precision worthy of *premiers danseurs*, under the glow of crystal chandeliers. Established in 1572, the school employs techniques dating from the time when horses were vital to military combat; proper training could determine whether battles were won or lost. The Baroque Winter School, where the horses strut and dance through the Grand Quadrille, was built in 1735.

MORE FUN:
Calgary Stampede,
Calgary, Alberta, Canada

Fun stampede

Horses are central to the attraction of the Calgary Stampede, a celebration of energetic cowboy culture. As well as rodeo events and chuck wagon races, there's a midway carnival and pancake breakfasts on a mammoth scale. The stampede takes place in July, though Stampede Park is open year-round, with attractions such as a casino, horse racing, and agricultural events.

Machu Picchu, **Peru**

Lost city of the Incas

The Inca city of Machu Picchu perches at an altitude of nearly 8,000 feet in the heart of the Andes. Built in the 15th century, it was an Inca stronghold for only about 100 years, although due to its remote location, the conquistadors did not sack it. Since 1911 and its "discovery" by American Hiram Bingham, its carefully crafted stone walls and buildings have fascinated the outside world, and it has been a popular destination with travelers.

MUST-SEE

The Palace of the Lost City,
Sun City, South Africa

Lost resort

Located in the crater of an extinct volcano and close to the big cats, elephants, and rhinos of Pilanesberg National Park, Sun City is a luxury gambling and entertainment resort. The Lost City Hotel is an architectural fantasy. Enter through a bridge flanked by life-sized statues of elephants and proceed to a variety of stunning and wildly entertaining attractions, including water rides through a man-made rain forest, pools with wave machines, and top-notch restaurants.

More Fun

Redwood National Park, California, USA

Gentle giants

Sequoia sempervirens, or the coast redwood, is the world's loftiest tree, reaching heights of between 300 and 350 feet and measuring 16 to 18 feet in diameter. Redwoods get old as well as tall: the oldest on record lived for over 2,000 years. Forty percent of the world's remaining redwoods live in the national park, which they share with a variety of fauna, including banana slugs, black bears, elks, cougars, and human visitors.

MUST-SEE

Lumberjack World Championships, Hayward, Wisconsin, USA

Cutting-edge lumberjacks

Since 1960, Hayward, Wisconsin has been a bad place to be a tree. This annual competition attracts lumberjacks from all over the world. Men and women, as well as mixed pairs (think "Jack and Jill sawing"), compete at events including tree climbing, log rolling, and speed races using buck saws, chain saws, and axes. Attended by 12,000 live spectators, this colorful competition is also televised.

Catacombs,
Rome, Italy

Religious underground

Beneath the city of Rome is a maze of passageways where Jews and early Christians buried their dead millennia ago. Forgotten for centuries, the catacombs were rediscovered by Romans in the 1700s. Many of these underground burial sites survive, and five are open to the public on a regular basis. In the sometimes elaborate gravesites carved from the soft rock, visitors can see ancient drawings with Christian, Jewish, and pagan themes dating from the tunnels' early days.

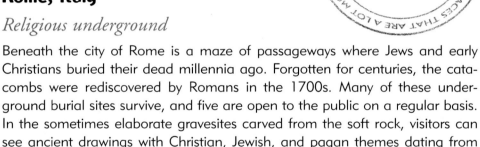

Cricova Cellars,
Republic of Moldova

Wine mine

Moldova, a wine-producing former Soviet republic, has
had some economic hard times, but does have one asset billionaires would
envy. In what was once an underground stone quarry is the world's largest wine
cave, containing a collection of about one-and-a-third million bottles in more
than 37 miles of passages. This underground treasure trove naturally provides
the perfect temperature and humidity for storing wine. Best of all, there are five
tasting halls, where visitors can sample the collection.

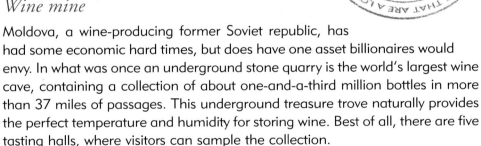

Stradivarian Museum,
Cremona, Italy

Red violins

It's still a secret. Nobody knows what instrument-maker Stradivari did to his instruments to make them sound as they do, but they sell for millions of dollars. Some think he used special wood, others a secret varnish. Stradivari lived and worked in Cremona in the 18th century, as did many other violin makers. The Municipal Museum there has a priceless collection of Stradivariuses and other violins, as well as tools and other artifacts.

Must-see

The Annual Cigar Box Guitar Extravaganza,
Huntsville, Alabama, USA

Cigar box blues

Anybody could make a guitar like this. In the early years of the 20th century, money was tight, and musicians built their own guitars, often using cast-off cigar boxes as sound chambers. The unique tone of these homemade instruments became central to the development of the blues. At the annual Cigar Box Extravaganza, fans can see a traveling museum of vintage cigar-box instruments, learn how to make one, buy instruments, and listen to lots and lots of music.

More Fun

To Jessica and Charlie

The author would like to thank friends and family who happily shared their ideas about fun, David Wondrich for Latin translation, and Barbara Paulding for help and guidance.

P H O T O   C R E D I T S

Copyright © 2008 AP Images: pages 1, 7, 9, 10, 13, 19, 25, 31, 35, 37, 39, 41, 45, 51, 57, 63, 64, 69, 71, 72, 79, 86, 88-89, 91, 95, 101.

Copyright © 2008 Photodisc/Getty Images: pages 20-21 (Tim Hall), 22 (Colin Paterson), 32 (David Toase), 36 (Neil Beer), 39 (Andrew Ward/Life File), 42 (Martial Colomb), 44 (Mark Downey), 46-47 (Sami Sarkis), 56 (John A. Rizzo), 59 (John Wang), 74 (Monica Lau), 82-83 (Neil Beer), 85 (Glen Allison), 92 (McDaniel Woolf), 94 (John Dakers/ Life File), 98 (Adalberto Rios Szalay/Sexto Sol).

Designed by La Shae V. Ortiz

Copyright © 2008
Peter Pauper Press, Inc.
202 Mamaroneck Avenue
White Plains, NY 10601
ISBN 978-1-59359-803-7
Printed in China
7 6 5 4 3

Visit us at www.peterpauper.com